I0274856

Bryan Davis

Combination Drills

Developed Scales in Odd Meters, Volume 1

For Trumpet and other Treble Clef Brass Instruments

AF001

© Copyright 2017, Airflow Music.
All Rights Reserved. Unauthorized Reproduction is Illegal.

ISBN: 978-0-9987280-2-5

Table of Contents

About The Author	3
Introduction	4
Technical Fundamentals	5
The Exercises In This Book	7

Exercises in 5/8 — 9

Exercise 1A - Major Keys	10
Exercise 1B - "Jazz" Minor	13
Exercise 1C - Harmonic Minor	17
Exercise 1D - Whole Tone	21
Exercise 1E - Diminished	25
Exercise 2A - Major	29
Exercise 2B - "Jazz" Minor	32
Exercise 2C - Harmonic Minor	36
Exercise 2D - Whole Tone	40
Exercise 2E - Diminished	44
Exercise 3A - Major	48
Exercise 3B - "Jazz" Minor	51
Exercise 3C - Harmonic Minor	55
Exercise 3D - Whole Tone	59
Exercise 3E - Diminished	63

Exercises in 7/8 — 67

Exercise 4A - Major Keys	68
Exercise 4B - "Jazz" Minor	72
Exercise 4C - Harmonic Minor	76
Exercise 4D - Whole Tone	80
Exercise 4E - Diminished	84
Exercise 5A - Major	88
Exercise 5B - "Jazz" Minor	92
Exercise 5C - Harmonic Minor	96
Exercise 5D - Whole Tone	100
Exercise 5E - Diminished	104
Exercise 6A - Major	108
Exercise 6B - "Jazz" Minor	112
Exercise 6C - Harmonic Minor	118
Exercise 6D - Whole Tone	124
Exercise 6E - Diminished	128

airflowmusic.com

About The Author

Bryan Davis is a trumpet and flügelhorn player and teacher, originally from the UK, now residing in New York City, USA. He has garnered an international reputation as a Lead Trumpeter, and is also highly regarded as a Jazz soloist.

He received his formal musical training at Leeds College of Music but considers "the road" as his true education. With over 25 years of professional experience to his credit, Bryan continues to learn from the thousands of musicians he has performed with around the world. His trumpet teachers include J. Brian Brown, Richard Iles, Gerard Presencer, Dick Hawdon, Brian Lynch and Roger Ingram.

In his early career, Bryan Davis was a longstanding member of the National Youth Jazz Orchestra of Great Britain. He also busied himself with a variety of Jazz and Commercial freelance work. Highlights included the Glenn Miller Orchestra UK, the Syd Lawrence Orchestra, the BBC Big Band, Phil Woods, Bill Watrous, Rob McConnell, Andy Prior Big Band, the Three Degrees, the Supremes, the Brasshoppers, in addition to numerous other big bands, jazz groups and production shows. In particular, the late '90s were spent with most of the greatest 'Latin' bands in the UK, as well as visiting groups from the USA and South America. These included Jesus Alemany, *Cubanismo*, *Sierra Maestra*, Isaac Delgado, Roberto Pla, Robin Jones and King Salsa, and *Salsa Celtica*. In addition, he played support gigs for Tito Puente and Tania Maria.

Bryan performed with a number of Theatre companies from 1999-2009, including: *42nd Street* (European Tour), *Cabaret* (European Tour), *The Official Tribute to… The Blues Brothers* (Europe & UK), *The Rat Pack - Live from Las Vegas* (West End, UK and Europe), *The Rat Pack - Live From The Sands* (US National). He is, perhaps, best known for his association with *The Rat Pack*, having toured regularly with them from mid 2004 to late 2009, and then occasionally up to early 2013. This was an important developmental period for him as a Lead Trumpeter.

The numerous European tours were spent largely in Germany and Austria. This led to his association with a number of groups from these countries, most notably Thomas Gansch's *Gansch & Roses*, the Lower Austrian Concert Jazz Orchestra and Otto Sauter's *Ten of the Best*, with which he still performs around the world.

In late 2009, Bryan Davis emigrated to the USA. Now a fixture on the scene in New York City, he has performed and recorded with numerous groups in the US including Arturo O'Farrill & the Afro Latin Jazz Orchestra, the Vanguard Jazz Orchestra, Orrin Evans' *Captain Black Big Band*, the Eyal Vilner Big Band, the Birdland Big Band, Charlie Rosen's Broadway Big Band, Mike Longo's NY State of the Art Jazz Ensemble & Gary Morgan's *Panamericana*, among many others. US theatre credits include sub work on Broadway for *On Your Feet* and *Book of Mormon*, and the National Tour of Legally Blonde.

Mr Davis has also become increasingly involved with music education, not only teaching trumpet lessons, in person and online via Skype, but also leading clinics and workshops, and appearing as a guest artist, around the world; at institutions including the University of Maine, NYU and Fullerton College in California, and at festivals including the 2014 Schagerl Brass Festival (Austria), the Wartburg Festival (Germany), the *Encuentro Nacional de Trompeta "Rafael Mendez"* in Mexico City (2012) and Puebla, Mexico (2013). Since late 2015 he has been an adjunct faculty member at The New School for Jazz and Contemporary Music, in New York City.

Introduction

These exercises are the combination of a tried and tested maintenance practice strategy and a new set of studies, originally developed for my own use, that have proved popular with, and beneficial for, my students.

The overall Combination Drills concept was something I hit upon on tour, early in my career, when I was touring regularly with "Broadway" type shows in Europe. Back at that time, I had yet to learn about efficient air use in playing the trumpet and so, in order to keep my chops together and maintain enough stamina to get through the gig every day, it became necessary to keep my daily warmup and maintenance routine to a minimum. This was particularly important on double show days! With some experimentation, I managed to trim my daily routine down to 20 minutes. This was achieved by identifying which trumpet techniques were targeted by particular exercises, then adapting how I was practicing those exercises, in order to work on a greater range of techniques. Effectively, I was covering about twice as much material and getting much better value out of my limited practice time. Later, when I was "off the road", it became second nature to apply the same principles to my daily practice. I discovered that I was now able to make quicker progress than ever before, because I was unifying different techniques which I had previously separated. Subsequently, I learned how to use my air more efficiently, and consider the airflow necessary to play a particular phrase or exercise, both moving from note to note, and in the overall arc of the phrase; at that point my growth increased exponentially!

The exercises in this book were born out of a deficiency I discovered in my musicianship as I started to become busier, here in New York. Namely, I found that I struggled to sightread and interpret music written in odd, and particularly asymmetric meters, e.g. 5/8 and 7/8. I describe these as asymmetric meters because the groove of the music is typically felt in larger beats of different length; e.g. 5/8 (5 quavers/eighth notes per bar) may be felt as though it's in 2, with one beat equivalent to 2 eighth notes/quavers followed by another of 3 (or vice versa), by comparison with a 4/4 meter (4 crotchets/quarter notes per bar) which is divided into beats of equal length.

Experience told me that this deficiency was largely an issue of familiarity (or lack thereof), so I took some material (scales) we all need to practice and maintain, and applied these meters to them. The result is a simple developed scale series which, if practiced according to my instructions, will allow you to work on the following technical and musical skills:

- Scales - all keys and in different tonalities. The exercises are notated herein in Major, so-called "Jazz" Minor (melodic minor ascending), Harmonic Minor, Whole Tone and Diminished scales.
- Finger/Slide technique.
- Slurring.
- Tonguing - particularly developing a gentle single-tongue approach which rides the airstream throughout long phrases.
- Unifying the airflow approach between slurring and tonguing.
- Connecting low and high registers.
- Stabilizing the embouchure throughout register changes.
- Developing breath support throughout long phrases and register changes.
- Use of Breath Accents, both while slurring and tonguing.
- Familiarizing oneself with less-common musical meters (time signatures) and the various rhythmic accent patterns used therein.

airflowmusic.com

Technical Fundamentals

Before the exercises themselves, and the specific instructions that pertain to them, there are a few Technical Fundamentals of Brass Playing that should be addressed. They may assist in playing the following exercises successfully and, if some of the techniques are not familiar to you by name, should serve to clarify the approach to the exercises that I prefer.

This is a brief list and contains only topics which are frequently misunderstood, or for which my approach may differ from "the norm." These are the basic explanations of certain concepts that have been most readily understood by the majority of my students. It should not be considered a "method" per se. Overall, I encourage efficient and musical playing by focusing on Airflow; getting smoothly from one note to the next, as well as from the beginning to the end of entire phrases. Since we are working with our air, the obvious starting point is Breathing.

Breathing

Breathing is one of the most fundamental physical actions we perform from moment to moment so, in some ways, it seems redundant to even discuss the topic. However, it is the main area where new students of mine have room for improvement, and most often the thing that is keeping them from playing as successfully and easily as they should be. This has proven to be the case with players of all levels, from beginners to professional musicians. To properly address it, it's necessary to discuss both the Inhale (breathing in) and the Exhale (the blow).

The Inhale

The breath we require to play a wind instrument is no different to the natural breath we take when performing any physical activity, at least as we inhale. However, there is a circumstance that gets in the way: as musicians, particularly when playing in an ensemble, we are required to breathe on somebody else's schedule! Therefore, we start to think about our breathing and that's when it tends to go awry. That's why so many "methods" of, or mnemonics for, breathing have become a part of the pedagogy.

When we breathe in naturally, while preparing for or engaged in physical activity, our abdominal area (stomach) does not significantly push out. Instead, we engage our core muscles and our chest raises up as our lungs inflate. This leaves us relaxed enough to move wherever we need to and prepared to make a smooth transition to whatever effort we are about to undertake; e.g. running, jumping, swimming, lifting etc, or playing a wind instrument. If we have breathed incorrectly and allowed our stomach to push outward (distend), then our breath support will be impaired as we attempt the controlled forced exhalation associated with blowing a brass instrument. The obvious symptoms of this are difficulty in playing long phrases, and a limiting of the extent to which we can (actively or passively) apply compression to the airstream as we change registers.

To find this natural breath, it can often be helpful to visualize oneself engaged in a favourite sport, or in another physical activity with which we are familiar. In sports, particularly, there is usually a preparatory moment when one takes a good breath; e.g. awaiting the starter pistol at the beginning of a footrace, preparing to serve in tennis, or preparing to dive into a swimming pool. I'm sure you can think of a similar example in your sport of choice. Placing ourselves there mentally can help trigger the automatic reflex to breathe naturally. Try it for yourself; close your eyes, visualize yourself in that moment, and breathe. You'll know if you've been successful (i.e. your core has engaged and your chest has raised); you will feel pleasantly full of air and free to move in any direction, at the same time.

There is one small tweak to this natural breath that I ask my students to make, in order to ensure a "deep breath". I characterize a deep breath not necessarily as a large breath (although it can be if the phrase to be played demands it) but, rather, as a breath with an open throat which encourages the feeling that the air is filling from lower down, or *deeper*, in the body. This is most easily achieved by breathing with the syllable "Oh", in mind. (Those familiar with the Star Wars movies may also liken it to the type of breath we hear from Darth Vader's respirator although, after the initial fun of the impersonation, we should breathe without the sound!)

The Exhale/Blow

Now we've taken in a natural breath, it's time to exhale. Of course, while playing our instrument, rather than simply breathing out we will be performing a controlled, forced exhalation. A common example of a forced exhalation is the action of blowing out a candle. Imagine you have a candle in front of you now (or light one if you have it handy), blow it out, and observe how your body performs this action. You will notice the same natural inhalation, described above, and a strong abdominal push to quickly expel the air. The way we blow a brass instrument is similar to this, albeit a slowed down and controlled version.

It is desirable to maintain good breath support while playing a brass instrument, as mentioned previously. After taking a natural breath, the core muscles engaging and the chest raising, breath support is enhanced by keeping the chest raised as we play through to the end of the phrase, despite the natural inclination to allow it to drop as the air supply runs out. This may feel a little awkward at first but, after a little practice, you should be able to accomplish it in a suitably relaxed manner.

It is worth noting that the quantity of air required to play a brass instrument is less than we usually think. We have been misled down the generations by instructions such as to "fill the horn with air." Since we don't exist in a vacuum, the instrument is already full of air! We simply have to move it at an appropriate speed, and in an appropriate quantity, to play the pitch, and volume, required. Most problems we perceive as insufficient embouchure strength, or the physical damage caused by excess mouthpiece pressure, can be instantly improved by simply blowing less air.

In order to find the correct amount of air to use, at least for the following exercises, I'd like you to start out by playing a 2nd line G (for trumpets and other treble clef instruments) or a 4th line F (for trombones and other bass clef instruments) at a comfortable medium-soft volume. Then, take your mouthpiece and without forming an embouchure, and keeping in mind the note you just played, simply blow some air through the mouthpiece. Experiment, varying the amount of air from blowing very hard to very gently, and find the spot where the air goes through most freely and easily, without any symptom of backing up. (Either that you feel it's backing up, or that you see your cheeks or neck inflate.) Now place the mouthpiece back in your instrument and play the note again, using this same quantity of air. You will probably find that you're blowing much more easily than before. This is the airstream I want you to use as you practice from this book.

Breath Accents

The concept of Breath Accents may be unfamiliar to many, but they are an important and useful tool in playing the exercises in this book. They are used to mark accents in slurred passages, as well to reinforce the gentle single-tongue approach we will discuss in the next section, in order to avoid articulating harder than is necessary and slowing down the tongue. They are effectively a small abdominal kick applied to a note, most similar to a short, hard laugh: "Ha!". Throughout this book, you will get plenty of practice in using them, as they will be necessary to mark the accent patterns of the exercises

Tonguing

For these exercises, as well as playing overall, I advocate the development of an extremely soft and *tenuto* single tongue. The articulation is a gentle "*Dah*" syllable, and I aim for consecutive notes to have only a beginning and no end. Practicing tonguing in this way helps to discourage stopping the air stream at each note, and makes for a smoother and faster single tongue, truly riding the airstream, which in turn allows us to play through lyrical phrases more musically. Once mastered, it then allows for a bouncier and crisper staccato "*Tah*" articulation, when you apply the same consistent Airflow approach. This tonguing is probably best demonstrated than described, so I will make a video demonstrating it, which will be available on AirflowMusic.com. This style of articulation also serves as useful gateway for jazz players to master "bebop" tonguing, which can basically be characterized as tonguing and accenting the second of each pair of notes.

For a more in-depth exploration of this type of articulation, particularly in terms of "bebop" tonguing, I strongly recommend the excellent book "*Modern Approach to Playing The Trumpet*" by Gerard Presencer, published by Warwick Music.

"Long Setting"

After gaining reasonable familiarity with these exercises, you are directed to play them as "Long Setting" exercises. This term will be familiar to anybody who has studied the Carmine Caruso method of Brass playing. In short, it means to play an entire exercise without removing the mouthpiece from the lips, and breathing through the nose as directed. This teaches the lips to make small adjustments inside the mouthpiece, rather than altering the entire setting when approaching an unfamiliar interval or register. Therefore, in general, Long Setting exercises start in an easy register of the instrument. In my opinion, it is of the utmost importance to try to maintain the same easy feel throughout the exercise, as found on the initial notes. Very often, I have students who are nervous to attempt Caruso-style exercises, because they have previously attempted parts of the method without the proper guidance, usually damaging themselves in the process. When playing exercises in this way, it is vital to listen to your body (and your sound) and **rest when you are tired!** Do not "power through" in the hope of building strength or a similar goal. This type of practice is about building the sort of agile, balanced strength a gymnast has, rather than the brute strength of a powerlifter.

The Exercises In This Book

There are six exercise patterns in this book, and each one has been notated in 5 tonalities. Each exercise is presented in **Major, "Jazz" Minor** (Melodic Minor Ascending), **Harmonic Minor, Whole Tone** and **Diminished** (whole step + half step) Scale versions. This gives a total of 30 Exercises, all notated in all 12 keys.

Exercises #1, #2, #4 and #5 are developed scales in Diatonic Seconds, Exercises #3 and #6 are in Diatonic Thirds (arpeggiations of the scale tones). (For the purpose of these exercises, I broadly define "Diatonic" as meaning "within the current scale" rather than strictly being a transposition of just the major scale.)

Alternating tonalities in each exercise are notated as 1) an expanding series moving each key away from the centre, and 2) following the Circle of 4ths.

In addition, the tonalities also cycle through the various rhythmic divisions or accent patterns appropriate to the time signature/meter they are in.

airflowmusic.com

In my own practice of these exercises, and in how I've asked my students to practice them, I set a series of goals for each one.

Goal #1

To begin with, practice each exercise slurred. Start out very slowly, ♪=60 (or slower if necessary), and aim to play smoothly and evenly throughout each phrase, resting at the double bar. Use a metronome to promote even tempo. Breathe where needed; keeping the mouthpiece in contact with the lips and breathing through the nose for as many beats as is necessary to take a full breath. Mark the accent patterns with Breath Accents. When playing these exercises very slowly, be mindful of your valve or slide technique. Good technique when playing slowly will pay dividends as you increase the tempo.

At the end of each key, rest for as long as you played. Ideally, practice with a partner and trade off playing each key.

Play these exercises at a soft dynamic, as marked.

Goal #2

Once you become more familiar with the application of the Breath Accents, gradually increase the tempo until you can play to each breath mark/double bar in one breath.

Be sure to play these exercises at a soft dynamic, as marked.

Goal #3

Practice each exercise slurred first time and tongued second time. Keep the tonguing as gentle as possible, a soft "Dah" articulation with no gaps between each note. Aim for the Airflow to be as similar as possible whether slurring or tonguing.

Keep the dynamic low, as marked. Try to maintain the same low dynamic regardless of register; effectively decrescendo-ing as you ascend, to back off on the air quantity in order to keep the volume down.

Goal #4

Apply the Breath Accents to both the slurred and tongued repeats of the exercise. Play each key as "Long Setting"; keep the mouthpiece in place throughout, breathing through the nose for as long as necessary at each breath mark.

Play the exercise as softly as possible, while maintaining a full tone.

Goal #5

Gradually increase the tempo until you can play each repeat in a single breath, then the entire key in a single breath. Practice each exercise marking each accent pattern for that meter.

By this stage, you can also change the pattern in which you play the 12 keys of each tonality, using the expanding pattern, Circle of 4ths, or a more traditional ascending or descending key order. You should also expand the register you play these exercises in. Perhaps set a higher starting note for the expanding series, or start to play some the lower keys up an octave during the Circle of 4ths. Be sure to keep the dynamic soft as you expand higher.

airflowmusic.com

Exercises in 5/8

The first 3 exercises are in 5/8 time. If you are unfamiliar with 5/8, be careful to play even eighth notes/quavers throughout.

There are two common accent/beaming patterns in this meter:

There are 15 exercises in the 5/8 section of this book (3 patterns, 5 tonalities on each). They are alternately notated with these 2 accent patterns, to help you become familiar with them. Ultimately, you should apply both accent patterns to all of the exercises.

Mark the accents with Breath Accents, while slurring to begin with. The Breath Accent is best described as a small volume kick to the note, achieved by a short, sharp abdominal push, similar to saying "Ha!" If you haven't thought about applying accents in this way before, you will probably overdo it to begin with. That's ok! Stick with it, and experiment with the severity of the accent, until you find a version that makes musical sense to you.

Once you've familiarized yourself with the Breath Accent while slurring, gently tongue the repeat of each exercise using a gentle "Dah" tongue, keeping the notes very connected, with no gaps between them. Try and get your tonguing as gentle as possible, so the slurred and tongued repeats of the exercise sound as close to the same as possible. Then add the Breath Accent to the tongue. It is best placed immediately before the "Dah", pushing the tongue faster and harder into the articulation, resulting in an accented sound, still with the same connectivity from note to note.

While using these Breath Accents, be mindful to keep the overall dynamic nice and soft. The marked *mezzo piano* is our maximum volume starting out with these exercises. Eventually, as they become more familiar, you should aim to play them as softly as possible. Our principle goal is to maintain a smooth, even airflow throughout each exercise, and have that airflow be the same whether we are slurring or tonguing. If we can train our lips to respond, in a relaxed manner, to a small and well focused airstream, then tone will be improved. We will also develop a much more consistent approach to playing easily and efficiently throughout all registers.

airflowmusic.com

1A - Major

Remember:
- Practice slurred to begin with. Start slowly - focus on playing smoothly and evenly in tempo.
- Once you're familiar with the airflow, tongue on the repeat. Tongue as gently as possible (think "dah") and *tenuto* (no gaps between notes.)
- Mark the accents with Breath Accents, whether slurring or tonguing.
- Play these exercises **softly** - maximum *mezzo piano* to start; and then as softly as they will speak, as you become more familiar with each scale.

airflowmusic.com

1B - "Jazz" Minor

1C - Harmonic Minor

airflowmusic.com

1D - Whole Tone

1E - Diminished

airflowmusic.com

26

28

airflowmusic.com

2A - Major

Remember:
- Practice slurred to begin with. Start slowly - focus on playing smoothly and evenly in tempo.
- Once you're familiar with the airflow, tongue on the repeat. Tongue as gently as possible (think "dah") and *tenuto* (no gaps between notes.)
- Mark the accents with Breath Accents, whether slurring or tonguing.
- Play these exercises **softly** - maximum *mezzo piano* to start, and then as softly as they will speak, as you become more familiar.

airflowmusic.com

2B - "Jazz" Minor

34

2C - Harmonic Minor

airflowmusic.com

2D - Whole Tone

airflowmusic.com

2E - Diminished

3A - Major

Remember:
- Practice slurred to begin with. Start slowly - focus on playing smoothly and evenly in tempo.
- Once you're familiar with the airflow, tongue on the repeat. Tongue as gently as possible (think "dah") and *tenuto* (no gaps between notes.)
- Mark the accents with Breath Accents, whether slurring or tonguing.
- Play these exercises **softly** - maximum *mezzo piano* to start, and then as softly as they will speak, as you become more familiar.

airflowmusic.com

50

airflowmusic.com

3B - "Jazz" Minor

3C - Harmonic Minor

airflowmusic.com

3D - Whole Tone

3E - Diminished

66

airflowmusic.com

Exercises in 7/8

The next 3 exercises are in 7/8 time. If you are unfamiliar with 7/8, be careful to play even eighth notes/quavers throughout.

There are three common accent/beaming patterns in this meter:

There are 15 exercises in the 7/8 section of this book (3 patterns, 5 tonalities on each). They are notated cycling through these 3 accent patterns, to help you become familiar with them. Ultimately, you should apply all 3 accent patterns to all of the exercises.

Mark the accents with Breath Accents, while slurring to begin with. If you've worked through the 5/8 exercises, then you should be familiar with the Breath Accent by now. If you decided to jump straight to the 7/8 exercises, here's the guidance about Breath Accents, and the overall approach to the exercises, which you may have missed:

The Breath Accent is best described as a small volume kick to the note, achieved by a short, sharp abdominal push, similar to saying "Ha!" If you haven't thought about applying accents in this way before, you will probably overdo it to begin with. That's ok! Stick with it, and experiment with the severity of the accent, until you find a version that makes musical sense to you.

Once you've familiarized yourself with the Breath Accent while slurring, gently tongue the repeat of each exercise using a gentle "Dah" tongue, keeping the notes very connected, with no gaps between them. Try and get your tonguing as gentle as possible, so the slurred and tongued repeats of the exercise sound as close to the same as possible. Then add the Breath Accent to the tongue. It is best placed immediately before the "Dah", pushing the tongue faster and harder into the articulation, resulting in an accented sound, still with the same connectivity from note to note.

While using these Breath Accents, be mindful to keep the overall dynamic nice and soft. The marked *piano* is our maximum volume starting out with these exercises. Eventually, as they become more familiar, you should aim to play them as softly as possible. Our principle goal is to maintain a smooth, even airflow throughout each exercise, and have that airflow be the same whether we are slurring or tonguing. If we can train our lips to respond, in a relaxed manner, to a small and well focused airstream, then tone will be improved.

The arpeggiations in Exercise #6(A-E) start to move further into the upper register. It is especially important to start these slowly, play softly, use good breath support and try to maintain the same easy feel from the lower notes, as you move smoothly from one note to the next. By not overblowing, you will allow the center of the lips to stay relaxed and let the notes respond, rather than trying to muscle and force them out. Rest at the slightest sign of pinching.

airflowmusic.com

4A - Major

4B - "Jazz" Minor

74

4C - Harmonic Minor

77

airflowmusic.com

4D - Whole Tone

4E - Diminished

5A - Major

5B - "Jazz" Minor

airflowmusic.com

5C - Harmonic Minor

5D - Whole Tone

5E - Diminished

6A - Major

6B - "Jazz" Minor

6C - Harmonic Minor

120

airflowmusic.com

6D - Whole Tone

6E - Diminished

www.ingramcontent.com/pod-product-compliance
Lightning Source LLC
Chambersburg PA
CBHW080345170426
43194CB00014B/2688